FREEDIVING MANUAL

Learn How to Freedive 100 Feet on a Single Breath

By Mike McGuire

Copyright© 2014 by Mike McGuire - All rights reserved.

Copyright: No part of this publication may be reproduced without written permission from the author, except by a reviewer who may quote brief passages or reproduce illustrations in a review with appropriate credits; nor may any part of this book be reproduced, stored in a retrieval system, or transmitted in any form or by any means – electronic, mechanical, photocopying, recording, or other – without prior written permission of the copyright holder.

Disclaimer: The information within the book "Freediving Manual" is intended as reference materials only and not as substitute for professional advice. Information contained herein is intended to give you the tools to make informed decisions about your freediving skills and ability to hold breath. Every reasonable effort has been made to ensure that the material in this book is true, correct, complete and appropriate at the time of writing.

The Author and Publisher has strived to be as accurate and complete as possible in the creation of this book, notwithstanding the fact that he does not warrant or represent at any time that the contents within are accurate due to the rapidly changing nature of the subject and the Internet (third party website links). Nevertheless the Author and Publisher assume no liability or responsibility for any omission or error, for damage or injury to you or other persons arising from the use of this material. Reliance upon information contained in this material is solely at the reader's own risk.

Any perceived slights of specific persons, peoples, or organizations are unintentional. This book is not intended as a substitute for the medical advice of physicians. Like any other sport, freediving poses some inherent risk. The Author and Publisher advice readers to take full responsibility for their safety and know their limits. It is also recommended that you consult with a qualified healthcare professional before beginning any training on the subject. Before practicing the skills described in this book, be sure that your equipment is well maintained, and do not take risks beyond your level of experience, aptitude, training and comfort level.

First Printing, 2014 - Printed in the United States of America

"Know your limits, but never accept them"

TABLE OF CONTENTS

Introduction	1
Chapter 1 – What is Freediving?	3
The Origins of Freediving	4
Freediving as a Competitive Sport	5
Official Recognition of Records	7
Freediving For Fun	9
Comparison Between Free and Scuba-Diving	10
Something For Everyone	11
Chapter 2 – Types of Freediving	13
Recreational Freediving	14
Competitive Freediving	15
Chapter 3 – Let's Get Started!	19
Understanding the Dangers	20
Before You Hit the Water	21
Factors to Consider	23
Chapter 4 – Breathing and The Mammalian Diving Reflex	25
It's Not Just Simply Holding Your Breath	27

The Basics of Better Breathing	29
Hyperventilation	32
'Empty Lung' Dives	33
Improving Breath Holding Ability	34
Maximum Breath Hold	39
Chapter 5 – Frame of Mind and Other Considerations	41
Relaxation for Freediving	42
Lifestyle Influences	44
Chapter 6 – Training for Optimum Freediving	47
Training Programs and Exercises	49
Chapter 7 – Swimming Techniques	57
Getting Under the Water	59
The Three Kicks	60
The Ascent	63
Chapter 8 – Equalization of Pressure	65
The Frenzel Maneuver	66
The Mouth Fill Technique	67
The Toynbee Maneuver	68
The Valsalva Maneuver	69
The Voluntary Tubal Opening (VTO)	70
The Wet Equalization Maneuver	70

Mask Equalization	70
The Dangers of Pressure	71
Chapter 9 – Freediving Equipment	73
Masks	75
Snorkels	77
Fins	78
Wetsuits	80
Boots and Gloves	81
Weights	81
Additional Equipment	82
Well-Known Brands	82
Chapter 10 – Safety	83
Preparation	84
Personal Awareness	86
The Role of the Buddy Diver	88
Additional Physical Effects of Freediving	90
Conclusion	91
About the Author	93

INTRODUCTION

Exhilaration or Zen-like calm. Both extremes are possible with the sport of freediving.

Freediving as a sport and leisure activity has been growing in popularity and for good reason. It can be the ultimate test of a man's physical stamina and mental focus or an extremely relaxing pursuit that provides yoga-like relaxation and the opportunity for deep meditation along with the feeling of being one with the beauty and majesty of the underwater environment.

Also called *Apnea* – from the Greek for 'without breathing', freediving is an ancient means of fishing and gathering the riches of the sea. Today, it is simply a form of swimming which involves submersion under water without the benefit of respiration equipment. In short, **freediving means staying under water as long as you can hold your breath**.

Many people freedive solely for the pleasure of the sensation of weightlessness and the ease of movement. Others enjoy sharing the underwater realms with the wide variety of marine life to observe and become a part of the ever-changing scene.

On the competitive level, athletes and adrenaline junkies push themselves harder and farther in one or more of the numerous freediving disciplines. Distance, depth and total time records with and without fins are maintained and tournaments are held around the world.

Freediving is also an important aspect of other pursuits as well such as underwater photography, spearfishing, synchronized swimming and more. The techniques used for breath control and focus in freediving also benefit scuba divers and surfers whose lives depend on maintaining presence of mind and the ability to equalize pressure in underwater situations.

Without the bulk or expense of gear and equipment, freediving is a practically pure pursuit of becoming one with the natural world of the sea. That is what you can achieve when you read this book and take advantage of the many hints and suggestions regarding the preparation for and practice of freediving.

You will learn about:

- Types of freediving – the different disciplines

- Training tips for strength, stamina and breathing

- Techniques for achieving the desired depth, distance and time underwater

- Safety practices and emergency response

- The difference between scuba and freediving

- Competitive and recreational freediving.

Join us and learn about the fastest growing water sport and how you can quickly and competently reach basic proficiency for freediving in as little as a week!

CHAPTER 1 – WHAT IS FREEDIVING?

"Freediving is about silence...the silence that comes from within..." – Jacques Mayol

The simplest explanation for **freediving** is that it **involves holding your breath while immersed in water**. Whether you are simply playing with the fish, trying to descend to depths over 200 meters, reach a particular length of time or cover a certain distance, you are involved in freediving.

Of course, there is much more to freediving than that.

The Origins of Freediving

Freediving dates back to the beginnings of man as is shown in cave paintings and in archaeological findings. As early as *7,000 years ago*, primitive man used freediving techniques to harvest clams from the sea bed and around 3,500 years ago pearls were collected for jewelry. Freediving for food and the items to trade such as sponges and shells has been part of life in many cultures around the world since then. Freedivers were even employed in ancient warfare to scout for underwater obstacles that would otherwise sink a vessel, to perform acts of sabotage or to retrieve anything that could be salvaged from shipwrecks.

Even in the modern day, many ports of call see the efforts of children who freedive for coins thrown from the decks of passenger ships and in remote locations, people fish and gather like they have for centuries. They begin as young children and develop the physical abilities to hold their breath and achieve significant depths and time of submersion.

Freediving as a Competitive Sport

The first freedive that was actually recorded occurred in water off of a Greek island where a ship had lost an anchor. An area sponge diver by the name of *Haggi Statti* was reputed to be the best diver around and was offered a reward to retrieve the anchor. After numerous attempts, Statti was successful and found the anchor at a depth of 88 meters. Using a heavy stone to descend, Statti located and was able to salvage the anchor with breath holds lasting roughly 3 minutes.

Using the same technique of weighting himself with a heavy rock, *Raimondo Bucher* wagered in 1949 that he could reach a depth of 30 meters (about 100 feet) on a single breath hold. He won the bet and began the modern sport of freediving.

During the decades of the 1950s and 1960s, competitive freediving grew rapidly with participants from all around the world. The techniques for preparation and breath holding were revolutionized first with the use of yoga and meditation practices then modern scientific analysis. The pioneers of the sport of freediving enjoyed competition for over 20 years, still diving well into their 50s. The 1988 film *The Big Blue* presented a fictionalized version of the story of two of these men, *Enzo Maiorca* and *Jacques Mayol* and created a new enthusiasm for the sport.

During the 1980s and 1990s, two new men took up the competition to be the best and reached unheard of depths of 130 meters and more. Because of the style of *Umberto Pelizzari* and *Pipin Ferreras*, a new discipline in the sport of freediving was created – the **No Limit category**.

Official Recognition of Records

SUUNTO VERTICAL BLUE
RESULTS
Day 4, 24/11/2012

national record
world record

Athlete		Disc.	Depth		Dive time	Card	Penalties	Points
			Announced	Realised				
Tomoka Fukuda	JAP	FIM	56	56	2:22			56
Alejandra Lopez	MEX	CWT	53	53	1:55			53
Alejandro Andres	ARG	CNF	51	51	2:21			51
Adriana B. F. Brandão	BRA	CWT	51	51	1:44			51
Kosuke Okamoto	JAP	FIM	50	50	1:53			50
Liv Philip	GBR	CNF	50	50	2:11			50
Alejandro Guedez	VEN	CNF	47	47	2:27			47
Gustavo Buss	BRA	CWT	47	47	1:19			47
Deisy Marquez	VEN	CWT	45	32	1:03	early	14	18
Macarena Benitez	CHI	FIM	45	45	1:45			45
Simon Bennett	CHI	CNF	42	42	2:16			42
Motoko Ishiwata	JAP	CNF	28	28	1:34			28
Alexey Molchanov	RUS	CWT	126	126	3:46			126
William Trubridge	NZL	CWT	126	108	2:59	early	19	89
Guillaume Nery	FRA	CWT	118	118	3:23			118
Ryuzo Shinomiya	JAP	CWT	100	100	3:08			100
Ant Williams	NZL	CWT	95	89	2:59		7	82
Rob King	USA	CWT	94	94	2:40			94
Mike Board	GBR	CWT	93	DNS				0
Rémy Dubern	FRA	CWT	92	92	3:12			92
Misuzu Hirai	JAP	CWT	87	87	2:45			87
Morgan Bourc'his	FRA	CNF	86	86	3:06			86
Mariafelicia Carraturo	ITA	CWT	79	79	2:54			79
Leo Muraoka	USA	FIM	78	78	3:04			78
Yaron Hoory	ISR	CWT	78	78	3:07			78
Nathan Watts	AUS	CWT	72	72	2:19	lanyard	10	62
Iru Balic	VEN	CWT	70	70	2:24			70
Carolina Schrappe	BRA	CWT	68	68	1:50			68
Yui Wada	JAP	CWT	64	50	2:03	early	15	35
Alejandro Lemus	MEX	FIM	61	61	2:57			61
Sam Barnes	AUS	CWT	61	53	1:48	early		53
Antonio del Duca	VEN	CNF	59	59	2:05	B.O.		0
Yuki Muto	JAP	CWT	58	58	1:43	B.O.		58
Junko Kitahama	JAP	CWT	57	54	1:48	early	4	50

Until safety and medical concerns forced the group to withdraw around 1970, the scuba diving organization CMAS kept early freediving activity records. Competitors did not stop trying to reach new depths and lengths of time but many achievements cannot be considered because there were no uniform guidelines. To make matters worse, several serious accidents hindered the growth of freediving.

To restore a consistent competitive atmosphere and offer clinics for instruction and the spread of the sport, AIDA (the *Association Internationale pour le Développement de l'Apnée*) was created in 1992. In spite of the efforts of other organizations, AIDA has become the leading group involved with the development and oversight of the sport. World-wide competitions were sanctioned starting in 1996 and continue today with AIDA unifying freediving within a membership of more than 65 different countries.

Freediving For Fun

Everyone that participates in freediving certainly does so for the fun and enjoyment of the sport but aside from competitive diving, many people rely on their freediving experiences for relaxation and pure pleasure. Some enthusiasts claim an almost metaphysical transformation as a result of the practice of breath control and relaxation for better diving times and the immersion in the undersea world of natural color and beauty.

There is a wealth of literature relating the immersion of a diver in water to the time spent in the relative comfort of the womb. Many comparisons are made to the mammals of the sea and the human ability to hold a breath that, with practice, allows the diver to remain under water for incredible amounts of time.

For many freedivers, knowing that their body is under their control is the ultimate thrill. That means that they master their fears and remain calm since a rush of adrenaline or sudden tension consumes precious oxygen. They believe that it is a meditative practice through which they look within themselves to conquer the supposed limitations of the body.

Comparison Between Free and Scuba-Diving

Both freediving and scuba diving share a common goal – to spend time under water. The difference is simple; **scuba divers use tanks of air** to spend as much time below the surface as possible whereas **freedivers depend on their own preparation and skill** to challenge the elements in shorter bursts of time.

Freediving is a much more intense experience than scuba diving since the goal is to push one's limits. Although the approach to underwater exploration and enjoyment is different, freediving and scuba diving enthusiasts experience not only excitement, but relaxation and even a sense of peace through their efforts.

Freediving and scuba diving are not mutually exclusive. The advanced training and breathing techniques learned for freediving help scuba divers swim with less effort and exertion and the skills learned for scuba diving such as equalization and maintaining calm under water are key elements needed by freedivers.

Something For Everyone

No matter what the reason may be to try the sport of freediving, it is simple to get started. The best features of freediving are the absence of equipment and therefore expense as well as the ability to perform it anywhere – from a backyard swimming pool to the most beautiful spots on earth.

As with any sport, however, you must follow some basic guidelines and always consider safety first.

CHAPTER 2 – TYPES OF FREEDIVING

Although mankind has participated in freediving for millennia as a means of survival and economic gain, there are two basic classifications for freediving today – **recreational and competitive**.

Recreational Freediving

Essentially, **recreational freediving is diving for fun**. In this respect, freediving is viewed as relaxing given the silence and intense feelings of peace that can be achieved underwater. It is also considered to be liberating in that the diver is not burdened with gear and equipment. There is no worry about decompression, no distraction from bubbles or noise and no training is really needed to get started.

For the best views of the most beautiful coral and exotic species of fish, you *don't need to dive deeper than 8 meters (30 ft.)* since light does not penetrate beyond that point. Humans possess the same 'diving reflex' that other marine mammals do which means that the heart rate slows, extra blood cells are released and the blood vessels in the skin and large muscles constrict preserving oxygen for the vital organs such as the heart and brain.

To accomplish this type of dive, most people can learn the basics and practice for as little as a few weeks. This results in the ability to perform a 45 second dive smoothly and easily so that you can enjoy the experience without much effort. The great part about it is that it does not require tremendous athleticism! The primary requirements for a successful dive are the proper frame of mind and technique – basically following a *few simple rules*: **remaining confident, keeping calm and conserving energy**.

Recreational freedivers are not interested in pushing the limits of their breath holding or distance. They do it simply to experience the beauty and relative weightlessness of the underwater world. Freediving does not necessarily mean descending to great depths so virtually anyone can participate as long as they are comfortable. The most important provision for safety in freediving is the presence of at least one other person who can assist in the event of a problem.

FREEDIVING MANUAL

Competitive Freediving

Since the first recorded freediving event in 1913, many records have been set and broken by competitive freedivers. Today, both *AIDA International* (International Association for the Development of Apnea) and *CMAS* (World Underwater Federation) maintain records and host events for freediving competition. In recognition of the growth of the sport and the variety of ways people approach achieving the best times, depths and distances, a number of different categories have been established with specific rules and guidelines.

Pool Disciplines

Three different types of competition most commonly take place in pools (with world record results as of February, 2013). These disciplines are also used as training activities for depth diving.

1. *Static Apnea* is the most basic form of competition in which the swimmer is timed for breath holding while remaining stationary holding onto the edge of the pool. (*Stephane Misfud*, France - 11 min 35 sec)

2. *Dynamic Apnea with fins* is a competition for distance while swimming on one breath with the use of bi-fins or a monofin. (*Goran Colak*, Croatia 273 m – 895 ft.)

3. *Dynamic Apnea without fins* is also a distance competition but without the assistance of swimming aids. (*Dave Mullins*, New Zealand 218 m – 715 ft.)

Depth Disciplines

Six separate categories make up the depth disciplines – 1 - 4 for competition and records and 5 & 6 for records only due to the dangers inherent in these styles.

1. ***Constant Weight Apnea*** requires the diver to follow a guide line to reach a depth they have previously declared without dropping any weights. This is accomplished with bi-fins or a monofin and the diver is not allowed to touch the line except to mark the depth of descent and begin the ascent. (*Alexey Molchanov*, Russia. 126 m – 413 ft.)

2. ***Constant Weight Apnea Without Fins*** follow the same rules with the exception of the use of fins or any other swimming aid. (*William Trubridge*, New Zealand 101 m – 331 ft.)

    This is considered to be the purest form of freediving and is also **the most difficult of the competitive disciplines** since it depends solely on only the diver's strength and training and requires the perfect execution of technique, propulsion, equalization and buoyancy.

3. ***Free Immersion Apnea*** also restricts the use of weights but allows the diver to use the line to pull himself down to depth and then back to the surface. For beginners in competition, this is **the easiest category** since the diver can control both the rate of descent and ascent as well as ear equalization. (*William Trubridge*, New Zealand 121 m – 396 ft.)

4. ***Variable Weight Apnea*** allows the diver to descend with a weighted sled then return to the surface by swimming with fins or pulling himself up the guide line. (*Herbert Nitsch*, Austria 142 m – 465 ft.)

5. ***No-Limits Apnea*** requires the use of a guide line to measure the depth a diver reaches by any means such as a sled. In this discipline, the diver can also use an aid such as an inflatable bag to return to the surface. (*Herbert Nitsch*, Austria 214 m - 702 ft.)

6. *'**The Cube**'*, otherwise known as the *Jump Blue** involves having the diver swim as long as possible in a cubic form that measures 15 x 15 meters at a depth of 10 meters for total distance (*Devrim Cenk Ulusoy*, Turkey 159 m – 522 ft.)

* An important note regarding *Jump Blue* is that it was designed as a competitive discipline that did not require diving to what are considered to be dangerous depths but the incidents of rescue for divers experiencing shallow water blackout have risen dramatically with this category in comparison to the others.

CHAPTER 3 – LET'S GET STARTED!

"The scuba diver dives to look around. The freediver dives to look inside"

The safest advice for anyone interested in learning how to freedive is to take a course with a certified freediving instructor. That being said, however, there are things that can be done to practice the basics needed for recreational freediving.

Understanding the Dangers

Before heading into the water, even the pool for practice, it is important to understand the importance of safety protocols. **Freediving should never be done alone**. Period. One of the biggest risk freedivers face is what is called *Samba* or *shallow water blackout*. This will be discussed in greater depth in the section about breathing technique and physiology but the key issue is that the pressure of diving affects the ability of the body to utilize oxygen resulting in the diver fainting as he approaches the surface. Without adequate supervision and a person on hand who understands the phenomenon and how to deal with it, death can result.

When it is time to actually freedive in the ocean, there are the same risks that all swimmers and divers face and freedivers can prepare for them in the same ways. Wearing protective clothing helps guard against sunburn, abrasions and the sting of jellyfish and other aquatic creatures. Common sense and swimming with a group reduces the risks presented by sharks and other predators. Of course, no one should ever engage in freediving under the influence of alcohol or drugs, especially since they affect the consumption of oxygen in the body.

As a reminder, this book is a presentation of basic information and should not be regarded as professional instruction or advice. The training and breathing methods presented are standard practices but the correct application of these techniques should be guided or judged by a certified instructor to avoid misunderstanding.

Before You Hit the Water

Let's work with the assumption that you already know how to swim. Even so, there are things you can do to prepare yourself for freediving before you ever get wet. It is said that knowledge is power so **learning** as much as possible **about breathing and swimming techniques** is a great way to gather information that can help you succeed. Watching videos and talking to experienced freedivers is also important.

The next step is to **check out the gear you will need** and get used to the feel and function of each piece. (Choosing gear will be discussed in *Chapter 9: Freediving Equipment*.) In a pool or even the bathtub, practice placing your face under the surface of the water to get accustomed to the ability to see, to ensure a proper fit and learn how to equalize the pressure in your ears. **In order to protect your ears from the pressure** experienced under water, you need to learn how to blow air against your pinched nose. That is done by applying pressure to the base of the nose piece with your fingers to seal off your nostrils and gently blowing. It often helps to wiggle the jaw or swallow at the same time just like you would to relieve ear pressure during a change in altitude such as when taking off in a plane.

Building stamina is another key component to successful freediving so exercises that include stretching and cardio-vascular fitness are recommended. Physical training, breath holding techniques and ear equalization will also be covered in more detail.

One last activity that can help prepare you for freediving is the form you need to **execute a clean surface dive**. Since there are really only two positions involved in freediving – horizontal and vertical to the water's surface – the most efficient surface dive is crucial to conserving oxygen and energy. To practice the basic movements, you can lie on a bed on your stomach so that your upper body is extended over the floor, balancing at your waist. Beginning with both arms extended out in front or tucked down along your sides, lower one arm straight down towards the floor and lift the opposite leg up, knee straight.

You can also practice this technique in a pool so that when you slip below the surface, you create as little disturbance on the surface as possible – just like an Olympic springboard diver executing a perfect dive. After propelling yourself forward with a kick for momentum, exhale deeply, inhale for maximum breath by spreading your shoulders out and back, bend at the waist and raise your leg. The goal is for a near vertical descent for the most streamlined movement through the water.

Prepared with this information and the assurance you gain from a bit of poolside practice, you are ready to experience the wonder of the undersea world. Now it is time to perfect your technique and develop the breath holding ability you want to achieve for either recreational or competitive freediving.

Factors to Consider

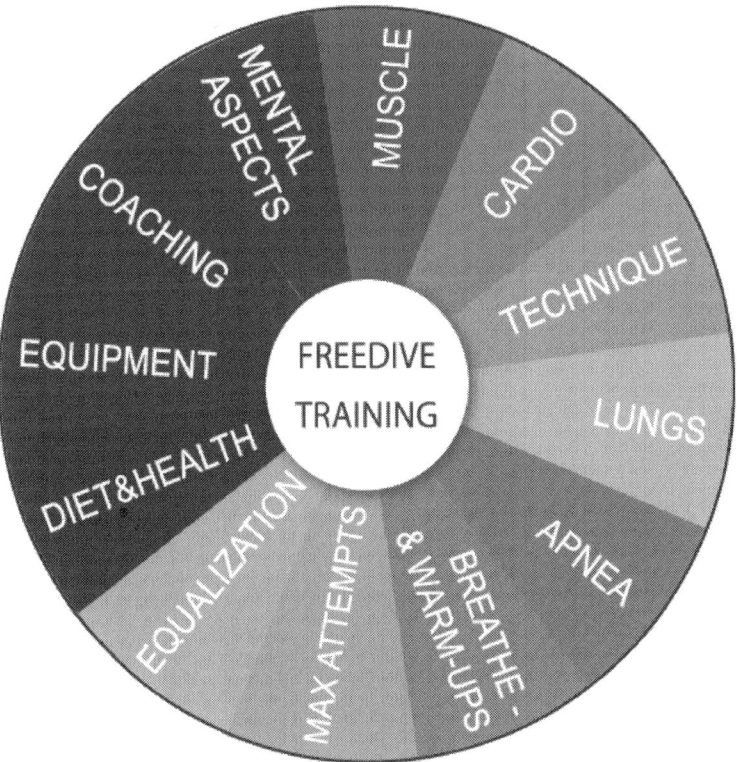

Anxiety and fear have no place in the water. You need to think about how you may react to certain things that can occur under water so that panic is not the response you end up with. For example, if you are not familiar with an underwater environment, you may be concerned about visibility and what you may step on or have brush up against you while you are submerged.

- **Learning** a little **about the location** where you plan to freedive is important so you know what to expect – the temperature of the water, the composition of the sea bed and the types of marine life that inhabit the area.

- **Becoming familiar with the gear** you will use is another key factor. You should be completely comfortable with the facemask and snorkel as well as the fins. Struggling – even just mentally - against these unfamiliar items saps you of critical oxygen and energy.

- **Remaining calm** is the most important element for successful freediving. Focusing on relaxing and moving gently adds to the length of time you can remain submerged without fighting for breath.

- **Swimming with an instructor or friends** who have experience with freediving provides support and guidance as you become acclimated to the differences between freediving and regular swimming or scuba diving.

- **Be aware of the different effects** the water, depth and time will have **on your body**.

1. After several minutes, internal pressure builds up causing diaphragmatic contractions and there is a strong desire to swallow what seems to be an increase in saliva in the mouth.

2. Contractions (similar to the feeling you get when you are going to be sick) begin – this is the body's way to encourage taking a breath.

3. Negative thoughts intrude trying to make you 'give up' and return to the surface. Hypoxic euphoria takes over making everything seem great – like you could go on forever. This is evidenced by the onset of tunnel-vision and sounds becoming muffled. Pushing past this feeling is dangerous – once you reach this point, it is time to turn and head for the surface!

CHAPTER 4 – BREATHING AND THE MAMMALIAN DIVING REFLEX

Many freediving enthusiasts refer to the beginning of our lives in the amniotic fluid of the womb to explain the natural ability that enables them to remain under water for extended periods of time. Even after birth and through infancy, a child will automatically hold its breath for 40 seconds and perform swimming motions.

Just like marine mammals such as dolphins, whales and seals, our bodies do amazing things when confronted with the underwater environment. In fact, the **human body can survive longer in the water without oxygen than it can on land!**

- Our pulse slows down to conserve oxygen (reflex *bradycardia*)

- Blood is reserved for the heart and brain (reflex *vasoconstriction*)

- The spleen releases oxygen-rich red blood cells (*splenic contraction*)

- The extremities cool to lower oxygen demand (*thermodynamic peripheral vasoconstriction*)

It's Not Just Simply Holding Your Breath

The science of breathing and human physiology is quite complex and depends on a number of inter-related factors. It is also extremely variable from person to person and even for one person on different days and under different conditions.

Barotrauma, or pressure related injury, is a very real concern for freedivers, especially as boundaries are pushed and new records are set. By simply submerging the face into water, the mammalian diving reflex is activated. This reflex is greater in colder water so temperature plays a significant role in the length of a dive and the ability of the diver to hold his breath.

Even the characteristics of pressure vary tremendously at different depths and on different bodies. Only 'empty' space can be compressed so **being able to clear the ears, sinuses and mask and protect the lungs is a critical consideration for all divers**. Damage to the middle and inner ear is common and the lungs can be compromised from repeated squeezing due to excessive pressures at the greatest depths.

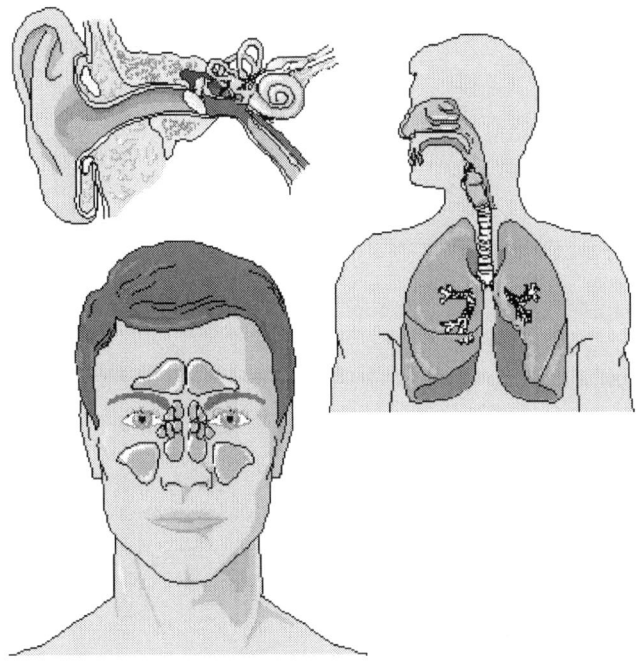

Just the physiological process of the metabolization of oxygen is a complicated factor since the body naturally produces carbon dioxide which builds up in the blood while oxygen is depleted. The high level of CO_2 triggers the reflex to breathe which is obviously impossible underwater and the release of pressure on the blood vessels as the diver rises to the surface can actually pull needed O_2 from the brain and other organs resulting in a black out.

It is vitally important to know your limits and to always use common sense while freediving because there is no warning that you are nearing the critical limit of available oxygen in your blood. **You do not feel anything to indicate that your oxygen is used up and most freediving blackouts occur in the last 10 meters as you return to the surface.** This is the primary reason for always diving with at least one other person – someone on the surface needs to monitor your ascent and be ready to provide assistance if you should experience a shallow water blackout or be afflicted with a loss of motor control which may prevent you from being able to keep your face out of the water. This loss of control is also called *Samba* because of the resemblance of the body's movements to a dance.

This is a serious safety concern and it should be noted that while there are actually very few deaths associated with freediving that are reported, some accidental drownings may have actually been the result of shallow water blackout. There have been several high profile deaths in recent years, however, among freedivers trying to set records so the possibility of shallow water blackout is something that every freediver needs to seriously consider.

The Basics of Better Breathing

Before you attempt to freedive or even perform breath holding training activities, **the first thing you need to work on is relaxation**. If the body and mind are not relaxed, oxygen will be used up quickly and inefficiently, motion will be wasted and the overall experience will not be enjoyable. Anything you can do to relax such as meditation, guided imagery and controlled breathing activities is helpful. In the water, anxiety can be reduced as you learn to freedive by focusing on the feeling of weightlessness, the silence and the beauty of the surroundings instead of the length and depth of the dive.

Breathing correctly has benefits for your entire body and well-being, not just your ability to freedive. These improvements in physiological functioning then allow for better freediving because the body has become more efficient in general. Proper breathing supports the nervous system, the digestive system, the muscles and energy levels, memory and concentration and the ability to get a restful, restorative sleep.

This 'proper' breathing moves a large amount of air in and carbon dioxide out of the lungs with little effort. Cellular respiration and the removal of waste products are also improved. Unfortunately, most people don't breathe this way, only using the top of the lungs with shallow chest breathing.

Abdominal breathing is deep and effective, expanding the entire abdominal cavity down to the pelvic region and up to the top of the lungs. This enables the body to take fewer breaths while it absorbs more oxygen and releases more waste products providing a calming, relaxing effect.

BREATHING OUT (EXHALING) WITH THE DIAPHRAGM

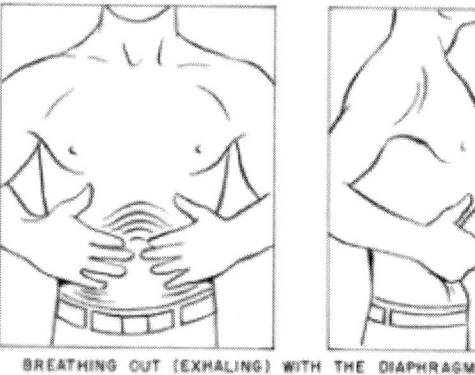

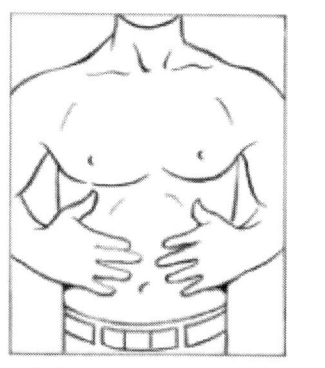

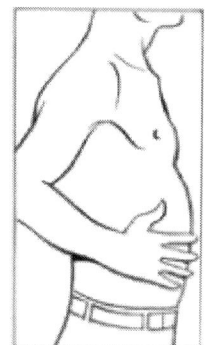

BREATHING IN (INHALING) WITH THE DIAPHRAGM

To practice deep abdominal breathing, try this exercise once in the morning and once in the evening, concentrating on the movement of your belly. The great part about this exercise is that it can be performed anywhere and does not require water or any special equipment.

- Stand up straight but comfortably with your feet slightly parted

- Relax and clear your mind (this is the hardest part!)

- Press your palms gently against your abdomen while your exhale through your mouth

- Hold your breath for a moment

- Smoothly inhale and focus on pressing your belly outward against your hands

- Hold your breath again for a moment

- Repeat this process for a total of ten complete breaths

As this exercise becomes more automatic, add more repetitions and take deeper, slower breaths.

Hyperventilation

Most people know what it means to **hyperventilate** - it's a condition in which you suddenly start to breathe very quickly. **Common misconception is that it can help a swimmer or freediver hold a breath longer.** This is not true and can, in fact, be quite dangerous. When hyperventilation occurs, the blood levels of CO_2 are significantly reduced. This postpones the reflex of taking a breath so oxygen depletion can sneak up on the diver before he is aware of it resulting in loss of motor control or shallow water blackout.

Even when not done intentionally, hyperventilation poses a danger to freedivers who are anxious, not well rested or are weakened for some reason such as too many dives or some other type of exertion. Hyperventilation and the resulting hypoxia (low air) also change the pH balance of your blood and can lead to heart arrhythmia and even death.

While the danger of hyperventilation is well documented, there are freedivers who use the practice as part of their overall training strategy to increase lung capacity. These techniques, though, are used by avid competitors and should not be considered by the casual recreational freediver.

'Empty Lung' Dives

A technique used by some deep-divers is the 'empty lung' dive which is accomplished through passive exhale. Instead of 'loading' the lungs prior to the dive, the diver exhales just to the point of a normal inhale response. There are several **reasons deep divers prefer this approach** in spite of the inherent dangers:

- The mammalian dive reflex is enhanced

- There is decreased buoyancy that improves the ability to sink to greater depths

- The reflex reversal of the normal dive response is limited so lung re-expansion is not triggered

- Nitrogen loads which can contribute to decompression sickness are reduced.

Improving Breath Holding Ability

Effective breath holding is a critical aspect for improving freedive times, depths and distances. It is an essential component of overall dive performance that involves the effective utilization of on-board oxygen stores and oxygen utilization, hypoxia tolerance and metabolic rate reduction.

Most highly trained freedivers work through established preparation sequences prior to any competition. These sequences include mental and relaxation exercises, physical stretching and breathing exercises. Variation is the key to **successful breathing practices** which **include static apnea breath holds of diverse lengths, deep purging breaths and hyperventilation.**

Because of the danger of deep or shallow water blackouts as a result of the failure to observe warning signals due to strong will and the competitive drive, these techniques should only be performed under careful supervision and the presence of rescue-proficient divers.

There are numerous exercises that can be performed out of the water to help build up lung capacity and the ability to hold a breath longer and more comfortably. Some are easy to do anywhere, at any time but you should always exercise caution since altering your normal pattern or depth of breathing can cause lightheadedness and lead to fainting. These are recommendations and don't guarantee success and you should not attempt them without understanding the consequences. The harder you plan to train, the greater the need to have someone else present who can help in the event of a black out.

Apnea Walking

This is a technique for increasing your breath holding ability that increases the body's tolerance for CO2, low levels of O2 and lactic acid build-up in the muscles. This activity can be performed on land as well as in the water. In either case, it should always be done with someone who is aware of the process and can react appropriately to the sudden onset of the loss of muscle control or black out.

- Sit with a straight back and your legs comfortably spread

- Place the palms of your hands on your knees

- Inhale and exhale deeply several times without hyperventilating

- Inhale deeply for a breath hold and hold for 1 minute

- Stand up at the end of the minute, still holding the breath

- Walk to a preset destination, concentrating on arriving at that point

- After resting, repeat the process lengthening or shortening the walking distance as needed.

Breathing through Straws

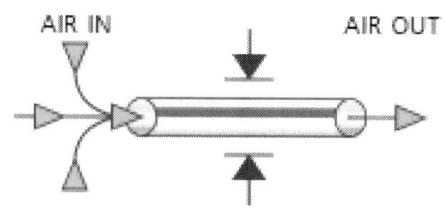

```
        AIR IN           AIR OUT
          ▽        ▼
        ⊳ )(==========( ⊳
                  ▲
          RESTRICTED AIR CAVITY
```

Breathing through straws is an easy way to train your lungs without an expensive air restricting device and can be done virtually anywhere. This type of activity strengthens the intercostal muscles that are found inside and outside the ribcage as well as builds the body's tolerance to CO_2 in the system.

Along with simply breathing through the straws/straw, you can do some simple exercises such as walking or jumping jacks to raise the heart rate and increase the breathing rate. Stop if you experience shortness of breath, hyperventilation or dizziness. Varying the types of activities you perform while breathing through straws or even just pursed lips is the key to building these muscles.

Another variation of this exercise is to inhale normally through your nose and then exhale immediately through a straw, pinching your nose gently to prevent any air from escaping. Take a few regular breaths and then use the straw again. Continue breathing like this in as natural a rhythm as possible for 4 to 5 minutes to start and try to add time each day to build up to 10 minutes.

Breath Training with an Air Restricting Device (ARD)

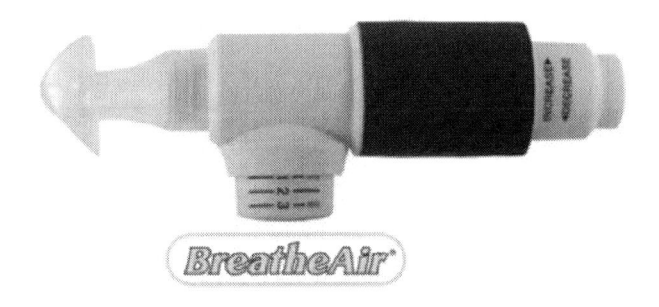

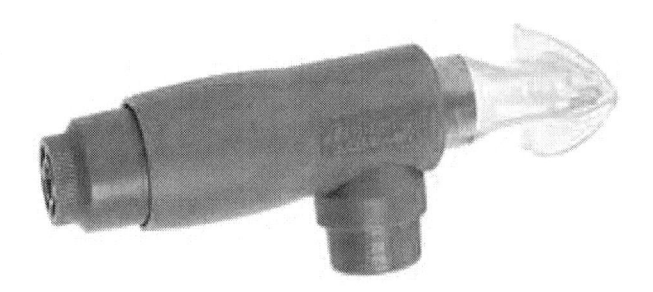

There are a number of ARDs on the market that are adjustable so you can select the appropriate level of restriction for practice. This makes it easy to gradually increase the resistance for better training or vary it for overall practice and maintenance.

You should begin an ARD session with several slow, deep breaths in and out. It is important to be relaxed, sit straight but comfortably and focus on diaphragmatic breathing without moving your chest or shoulders.

- At the top of a deep breath, place the ARD in your mouth and exhale as long, as hard and as much as you can.

- At the bottom of the exhale, remove the ARD and forcefully expel the rest of your air.

- Immediately replace the ARD and inhale as long, as hard and as much as you can.

- At the top of the inhale, remove the ARD and continue to inhale to top off your total capacity.

- Hold this breath until the lightheadedness passes or for 15 seconds – whichever comes first.

- Replace the ARD and again exhale as long, as hard and as much as you can.

This is the pattern you should follow to build up to 30 complete breaths – 30 inhales and 30 exhales – twice a day, every day. Please remember to use common sense and caution!

Maximum Breath Hold

Breathing is a natural phenomenon so most people don't know how long they can actually hold their breath. For a healthy individual, it should be possible to hold the breath for 1 ½ to 2 minutes. The good thing about breath holding, though, is that with training, it is possible to significantly improve that ability. The most difficult part of extended breath holding is forcing yourself to ignore the body's natural signals for the need to take a breath. Muscle spasms attempt to prompt your lungs to exhale and it takes practice and mental preparation to overcome this warning.

Caution is important for all breath holding practice because repeated oxygen deprivation can have negative effects on the body when that training takes place out of the water.

CHAPTER 5 – FRAME OF MIND AND OTHER CONSIDERATIONS

Mental strength and peace of mind are crucial elements for every freediver. Without these psychological traits that allow the diver to control his natural reflexes, all the training in the world will not help a diver achieve success. For truly rewarding underwater experiences and the attainment of depth, time and distance goals, freediving requires an overall lifestyle commitment.

Not only are physical fitness and technique important, general health considerations in terms of diet, rest and mental attitude also affect the body's functions and ability to freedive, even to the point of inhibiting the mammalian dive reflex. Anything that can help the body to function at optimal efficiency is a benefit to a freediver.

Relaxation for Freediving

Yoga and Meditation

In addition to (or as a logical follow-through of) breathing exercises, yoga is a terrific way to prepare for the rigors of freediving. For thousands of years, yoga has enabled its practitioners to focus their mental and physical abilities so that the mind and body work as one in calm and unity. The spiritual peace associated with the discipline of **yoga leads to more efficient oxygen consumption** which is crucial for longer dives.

There are numerous yoga practices but the basics contribute to physical strength and fluid motion, the subtle awareness of the body and its needs including breath control and the development of core strength, control of the nervous system and a more complete mind-body connection.

Whether through yoga or some other type of meditation, visualization and concentration aid the freediver in learning specific physical skills and developing all around confidence. Although the concept of concentration seems to be opposite to the idea of relaxation, it is through the focused concentration of meditation that allows for the inherent understanding of the art of freediving. It removes fear and provides the trust in ourselves that allows us to stay in the moment at each step of a dive.

Without the control of the mind that comes from meditation, the mind controls the body and fears and doubts can set in. Meditation allows you to remain fixed in the reality of the dive, fully experiencing every move and view while trusting your training and technique. Instead of focusing on a specific goal, you stay in tune with all the functions of your body and the environment through which you intuitively know when to ascend.

Deconcentration of Attention

Introduced in the 1980s, the deconcentration of attention is a mental process by which the individual aspects of a person's consciousness are blended together into a uniform field enabling the person to see 'the whole picture'. Instead of focusing on a particular item, the mind takes in all sensory information simultaneously.

Freediving involves the constant monitoring of not only the body and its oxygen supply, CO_2 concentration and level of exhaustion but also the various external conditions such as temperature, current, predators and more.

It is critical to be able to recognize and calmly respond to any factor that is not expected.

One key difference between attention deconcentration (AD) and meditation is the retention of a connection with the current reality. Meditation allows you to relax your mind and body so there is no real point of focus but AD keeps you entirely in the present although free of emotional reactions. This prevents sudden adrenaline bursts or other physiological effects that influence the body's function.

Lifestyle Influences

There is no doubt that freediving, especially for competition, requires a tremendous level of dedication and attention to the optimum functioning of the body. In addition to proper fitness, increased breathing ability and a controlled frame of mind, other aspects play a role in preparing for success.

Diet

Proper diet is a key element in the efficiency of the human body. Some diving enthusiasts may claim that a vegetarian diet is the best while others insist on the necessity of meat proteins, but a **well-balanced diet** with as many natural foods as possible is the safest choice.

For training purposes and getting ready for a competitive event, there are some **general guidelines** that have proven to be effective.

- Abstain from alcoholic beverages for at least one month for greater energy and muscle efficiency.

- Cut out caffeine at least 2 weeks prior to competition to lower your daily average heart rate as well as improve hydration.

- One week ahead of an event, cut out dairy products that can increase mucous and make it more difficult to equalize.

- The last several days should be free from processed meat, refined sugars and products high in gluten since they require more work from the digestive system.

- Focus on a variety of healthy carbs such as rice and iron-rich foods such as dark poultry meat and leafy greens like kale and spinach.

- Remain hydrated, preferably with water, all day every day. Even slight dehydration takes a significant toll on muscle performance, mental alertness and the build-up of 'wax' in the ears that makes equalization more difficult.

Rest

Even during intense training, it is important to observe your body's rest requirements to ensure improvement without injury. After pushing yourself to any extreme, you need to allow your body to rebuild and recuperate. Take advantage of 'off' days by treating yourself to a massage or other special treat, meditate, eat healthy foods and appreciate the effort you are making to excel.

While freediving, it is possible to spend all day enjoying the experience but between dives, **you should rest twice as long as you spent performing your previous dive**. The key is to avoid exhaustion or muscle strain and that means that every dive and every day will be different.

CHAPTER 6 – TRAINING FOR OPTIMUM FREEDIVING

In order to improve breath holding performance, anyone can engage in the basics as long as it is done slowly and gradually in the presence of a buddy. The aim is to encourage better performance – not force it!

You will start by gathering some statistics and making note of them:

1. Hold your breath underwater – time it and record the result
2. Take your pulse and record the rate
3. Measure how deep you can dive on one breath and record it

Now you will **work on improving those numbers**:

1. Take deep, slow breaths exhaling slowly, twice as long as you in-

haled (breathing in and out at the same rate results in hyperventilation)

2. When this is comfortable, have someone else record your pulse rate

3. After you are able to maintain this type of breathing at a pulse rate lower than 80, go to the spot you took your original diving measurement and try to add 2.5 m (10 feet)

4. Work at this rate until it is comfortable and then add another 2.5 m.

After about a month, your pulse should be 60 or lower and your distance improving. Just as with any exercise program, progress takes time and patience. Pushing too hard, too fast can lead to injury so it is important to maintain gradual improvements. Gradually increase the demands you make on your body, work with them until they are comfortable and relatively simple then add more.

The combined effects of all aspects of training – breath holding, lung capacity, relaxation, equalizing, technique and physical fitness and strength – make it possible to achieve better results in the water.

Training Programs and Exercises

For the best results as a freediver, it is important to undertake a physical training program that incorporates **cardiovascular exercises, cardio high-intensity activity and muscle or strength training**. The purpose is to develop a strong heart, low resting pulse rate, good tolerance to the presence of CO_2 and lactic acid in the system and muscles in the right places that function in an efficient manner.

To reach this type of readiness, a varied workout involving a number of different activities and difficulties is required. Cross training provides many excellent rigorous pursuits that can offer plenty of enjoyable exercise. If you break down a year into quarters with one being devoted to competition or active freediving excursions, the other 3 quarters can be divided into:

1. General training to build overall strength and cardio fitness

2. Intense training which focuses more on increasing lactic acid tolerance, building specific muscles and stretching particular areas, and

3. Specialized training for specific disciplines and increasing your breath holding ability

Interval Training

No matter which types of activities you choose for working out, the best approach is with interval training. Coaches in all types of sports recommend interval training because it increases the athlete's ability to exercise longer and perform better at varying intensities. With the inclusion of high intensity bursts, the metabolism is boosted and this is a tremendous benefit for the conservation of oxygen.

Running

For the development of leg muscles and great cardio vascular improvement, long distance and shorter high intensity runs work very well. Vary the lengths, intensities and distances you run over the course of each week for the best results. Be careful, though, since running is considered high impact and you don't want to injure your feet, ankles or knees. Roller blading, ice skating and dancing are also activities that benefit both the muscles and cardio efficiency.

Swimming

Just like with running, swimming different distances, speeds and total times provides a very effective workout. Swimming also provides an opportunity to work the entire body while using a kickboard allows you to focus on the different types of kicks. Including time to swim with fins helps to maintain muscle memory specific to freediving and the types of kicks used to propel you to the bottom and back up to the surface.

Cycling and Rowing

These two activities allow for variation in the overall exercise program while still focusing on cardio strength. Cycling obviously builds leg muscles and can lead to good practice dealing with lactic acid build up while rowing works the chest, back and shoulders for increased lung capacity and core muscle development.

Weight Training

Using free weights, machines or even your own body weight offers another way to build muscle and improve the neurological reactions within the muscles when diving. Instead of building muscle mass with heavy weights, try lighter weights with more reps for lean muscle. Several different leg exercises work the same muscles needed for diving and can be done anywhere at any time.

- **Leg raises**: Lie on your back with your arms stretched out on the floor straight over your head or at your sides. Raise one leg about one foot off the floor, hold for a few seconds and slowly return the leg to the floor. Alternate legs and try to increase the total number of reps over the course of the week.

- **Bent-knee leg raises**: Starting on your hands and knees with a straight back, raise one leg while maintaining the 90° angle. Raise the knee as high as possible, clenching the buttocks as you do so. Alternate legs for a total of 15 reps with each leg.

- **Squats**: With your feet shoulder width apart, back straight and head up, slowly squat down until your upper thighs are virtually parallel to the floor. Pause and then slowly straighten up.

- **Calf lifts**: Stand on the balls of your feet on a step or curb and smoothly raise and lower yourself using the muscles in the calves. Lowering your heels below the level of your toes is a great bonus with this exercise. This can be combined with a stepping activity to not only work the muscles but also increase cardio strength.

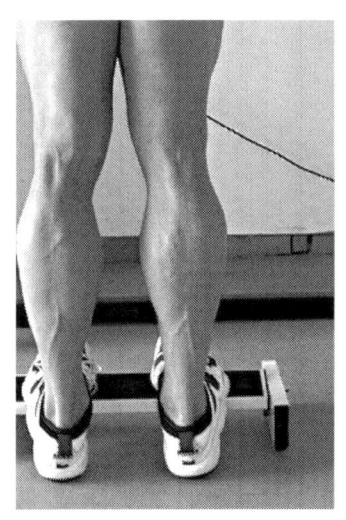

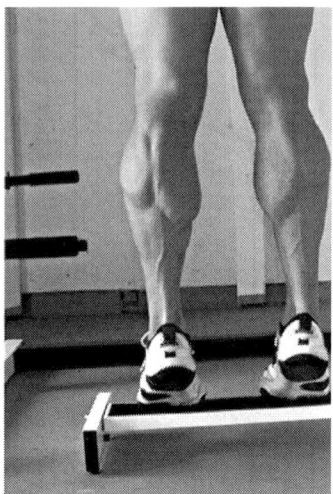

Core Strength

More than just the abs, the core is a group of at least 10 different muscles that extend from the pelvic floor to the shoulder girdle. These muscles work together to provide support, balance and stability to the spine, trunk and torso that allow the extremities to generate powerful movements. For freedivers, especially those who choose to use a monofin, a strong core helps maintain balance, a hydrodynamic form and the ability to perform the dolphin kick more effectively.

Many different exercises work the core muscles and can be enhanced with the use of equipment such as kettlebells, medicine balls, stretch bands and stability balls. The key is to work several different core muscles at the same time. The great thing about building core strength is that it can take as little as a 15 to 20 minute workout 3 or 4 times a week and can be incorporated into practically any workout routine. Basics include *planks, v-sits, lunges* and *twists*, all of which are part of Pilates and many yoga positions.

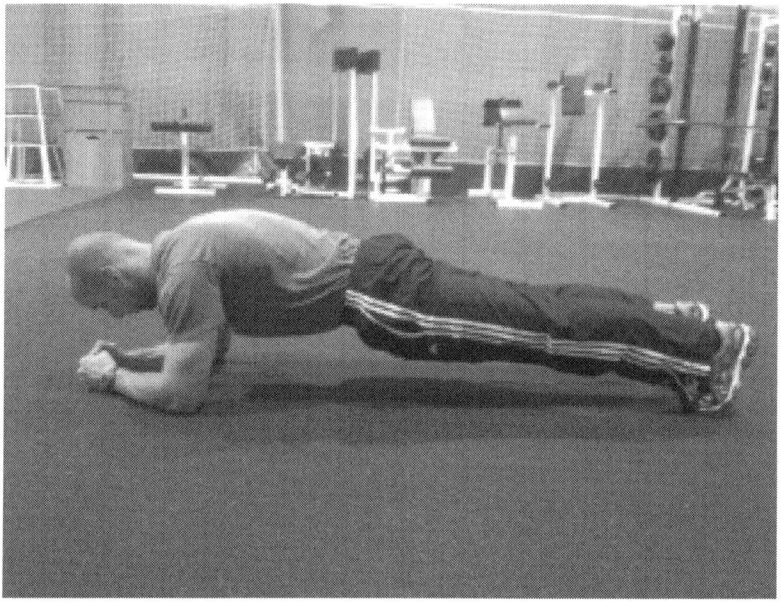

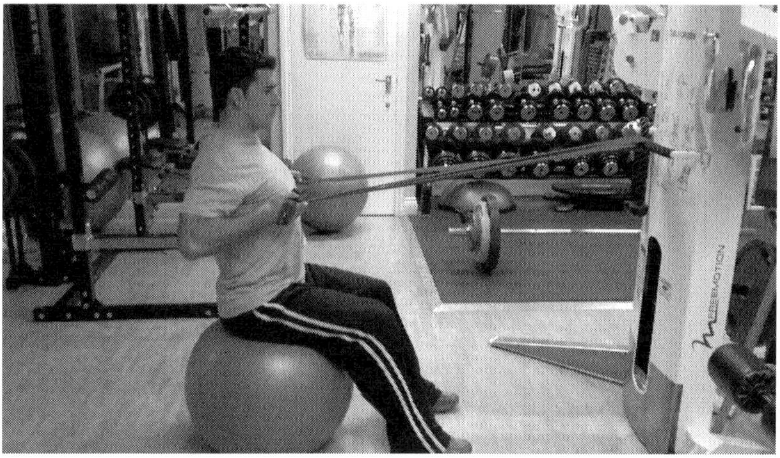

Aerobic and Anaerobic Training

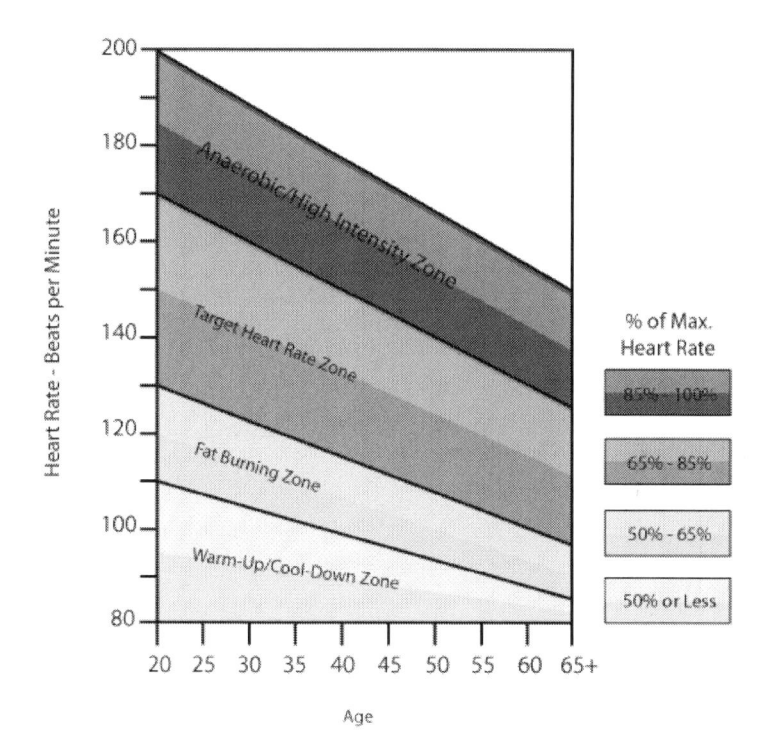

Aerobic training is simply exercise with the presence of oxygen and consistent practice allows for more activity with a lower heart rate. This maximizes the amount of oxygen in the blood and allows for better transport of that oxygen to the heart, lungs and brain. **Anaerobic training** is working the muscles without fresh O2, usually at 80 – 90% of maximum heart rate. This is when the body has to function in the presence of greater levels of CO2 and lactic acid.

With caution and a careful observer, many of the land activities can be done in connection with breath holding to build up anaerobic function. Such activities are considered '*dry apnea*' and are crucial for the most efficient response to the prolonged lack of O2 experienced by freedivers. This can be quite dangerous and you should never push your limits breath holding while doing any other activity.

CHAPTER 7 – SWIMMING TECHNIQUES

Swimming, or more accurately, finning techniques used by world class freedivers are economical in terms of the amount of movement and effort expended due to the need to conserve oxygen. This is the reason for a strong core and well-developed leg muscles. The **goal is to be as hydrodynamic as possible** to reduce drag and prevent the disruption of water flow over the body.

One of the most important considerations while freediving is the **position of the hands**. For the descent, the arms should be closely in line with the body. When using a hand for equalization, the elbow should be as tight to the rib cage as possible and any change of position should be made with as little excess or sudden movement as possible.

The head should always be in line with your body and facing straight ahead.

Getting Under the Water

When you are freediving for depth, the most important part of the dive involves smoothly getting your body underwater into a freefall. After you are relaxed on the surface in a 'dead man's float' or the fetal position and have taken your final deep breath, you can perform a duck or surface dive to bring your body into a vertical line.

Just as with springboard diving, **the goal is to create minimal disturbance to the surface of the water** – not for any other reason than the smoothness and simplicity of the motions that conserve energy and oxygen.

- Beginning on the surface with your arms extended in front of you, bend at the waist and point your arms to the floor of the pool or ocean. You may begin with a few strong kicks for momentum prior to bending your arms.

- Raise one leg to cause your body to sink and use your strong core muscles to lift both legs in a vertical line.

- Take a strong swimming stroke with your arms and lay them back along the sides of your body where they should remain except for equalization.

- By this time, both fins should be submerged so you can begin to kick.

The Three Kicks

Flutter Kick

This is the most common finning technique because of its power. This kick involves straight legs (as much as possible) and long, gentle strokes powered primarily by the muscles in the front of the thighs. The motion is the virtually the same as that used by free-style swimmers and provides the greatest propulsion while keeping the body streamlined. The downward stroke of the flutter kick is the driving force so the longer the stroke, the more time the fins have to push the swimmer forward. This kick is used for both the descent and ascent when speed or the need to cover a great distance is required.

Frog Kick

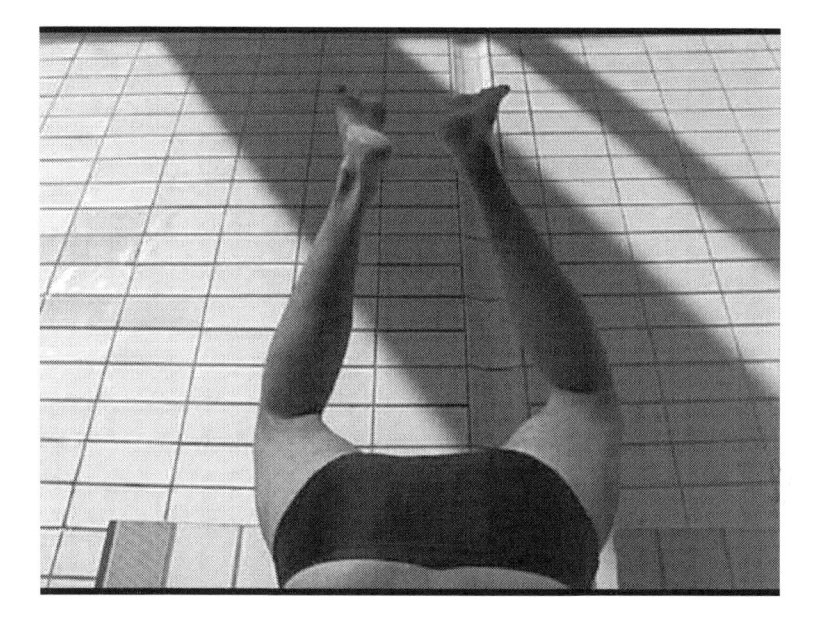

The frog kick, which is essentially the same as the breast stroke kick, is used mostly as means to rest the muscles used in the flutter kick. It is also the preferred finning technique when swimming along the bottom of the sea so that the silt is not disturbed and visibility reduced. It also allows the diver to remain more stable while moving forward unlike the flutter kick which involves a gentle side-to-side twist of the body. The frog kick is effective for a kick and glide form of propulsion.

Dolphin Kick

By itself, practicing the dolphin kick is a great way to build up core muscle strength and flexibility. It is used by competitive swimmers for power after making turns except when performing the breaststroke. The key to successfully performing the dolphin kick is fluidity of motion along the entire length of your body. Several steps blend together to accomplish this style of finning that is roughly the equivalent to cracking a whip.

- Swim with your head directly in line with your body and your arms along your sides

- Beginning with your core, press your midsection downward

- Follow through with this movement by rotating the hips forward

- The 'wave' continues through the knees which are not locked but bend slightly to transfer the motion to the feet

- 'Snap' the whip by fully extending your ankles and pointing your toes

The Ascent

When it is time to return to the surface, assume a streamlined vertical position with your arms extended above your head and hands together. Keep your head in line without looking either up or down and kick with strong, purpose- full strokes. This is the most dangerous part of any dive because of the possibility of shallow water blackout so your buddy or spotter needs to be quite vigilant.

CHAPTER 8 – EQUALIZATION OF PRESSURE

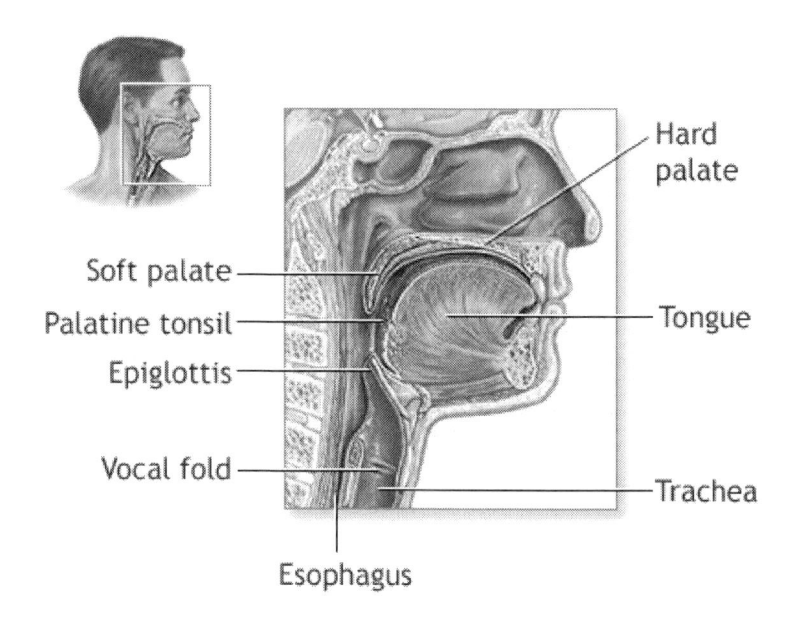

Although equalization is related to breathing technique, its importance is such that it deserves special consideration. Without proper equalization, divers could not have reached the depths that are now possible without significant damage to the ear drums, sinuses and even the skull.

There is a very simple rule to remember regarding equalization – **perform it frequently and definitely before you begin to feel any pain!**

The Frenzel Maneuver

As unlikely as it may sound, this is a technique that was devised for dive bomber pilots in World War II who suffered from the increased atmospheric pressure they encountered when landing their planes. Once you learn it, the Frenzel Maneuver becomes quite natural and is easy to perform. The basic idea is to **compress the area between the glottis and the lips and nose** in order to minimize the amount of oxygen needed for equalization at greater depths.

Please note – for practice on dry land, do not completely close off the nose – pinch only one nostril!

- Pinch the nose and close your mouth

- Close your epiglottis (raise the back of your tongue and close your throat)

- Press your tongue against the roof of your mouth in back of your teeth to create a seal. This is called a T-lock.

- Use your facial and throat muscles to compress the airspace in your mouth.

- Push your tongue up inside your mouth to make a K-lock (the tongue flattens along the roof of the mouth toward the back).

- Maintain a neutral position of the soft palate so air can reach the opening of the Eustachian tubes and the sinuses and allow the air to fill them.

- Re-load the air in your mouth by opening then closing the epiglottis.

The Mouth Fill Technique

This equalization technique takes advantage of the air that is held in the mouth and throat to provide an air reserve. You start with the Frenzel Maneuver and access air from spaces that are not as highly compressed as the lungs and move the air held in your cheeks to the ears and sinuses by utilizing the muscles of the head, tongue and jaw. You can **use this technique at 10 feet or wait until closer to 25 feet** but it must be done before you hit residual volume or it will not work.

To be truly effective, the process should be practiced and mastered on dry land before attempting to use it in the water. This is to avoid swallowing the reserve air into the stomach or losing it through an incompletely sealed mouth. Although the procedure is not really complicated, there are a number of **steps that need to be performed in the correct order** in order to achieve success. Complete confidence gained through practice is a key component to the ability to use this technique.

- Extend your lower jaw forward

- Pinch your nostrils closed

- Keeping your lips sealed tight but your teeth apart, fill your cheeks with air

- Close off your epiglottis

- Maintain an open soft palate

- As you continue to descend, bring your chin back into a normal alignment

- Compress the air further by closing your mouth (bringing your teeth together)

- Use your tongue and the muscles in your throat and neck to compress the space even more

- 'Suck in' your cheeks for maximum compression

The Toynbee Maneuver

This is probably something everyone has done at some point in their life – when ascending a mountain in a vehicle or taking off in a plane. It simply involves pinching the nose closed and swallowing, resulting in the Eustachian tube being pulled open and air moving into the space to create equalization. The significant concern with this technique is the presence of a sufficient gradient of air pressure for equalization to occur.

The Valsalva Maneuver

Effective only up to depths of 30 meters, this equalization technique was first performed in the 1700s. It is quite simple to do and can be repeated as often as needed as long as there is air in the lungs. It is not a preferred technique, though, since it involves the contraction of the lung muscles and that consumes oxygen.

- Pinch the nose closed either with the forefinger and thumb or press against the base of the nose piece on the face mask.

- Try to blow air out through your nose.

- You have succeeded when you hear a thumping noise.

The Voluntary Tubal Opening (VTO)

Developed by the French Navy in the 1950s, this is a difficult technique to learn and use reliably. It takes considerable preparation and practice that lasts for four weeks of daily exercises for the tongue, roof of the mouth, the Adam's apple and the jaw. Due to the stimulation of the alimentary canal and possible feelings of nausea, these exercises should be done in the morning on an empty stomach.

Consult the *IFA manual for BTV* (VTO) for full instructions.

The Wet Equalization Maneuver

Another extremely difficult maneuver is the Wet Equalization Maneuver in which water is allowed to enter the sinuses and middle ear. This effectively cancels out the pressure differential so no air is needed. The danger of this is the possible aspiration of water into the lungs which could result in drowning. Even without such a significant problem, this method frequently leaves the diver with infections in the ears and sinuses.

Mask Equalization

A small amount of air escapes from the nose when the Frenzel or Valsalva Maneuvers are performed and that may be enough to equalize the pressure on the mask. If not, however, it may be necessary to blow some air out the nose. This can be a problem at deeper depths due to the pressure on the lungs decreasing available air volume. For this reason, many divers simply do not use masks or use fluid goggles.

The Dangers of Pressure

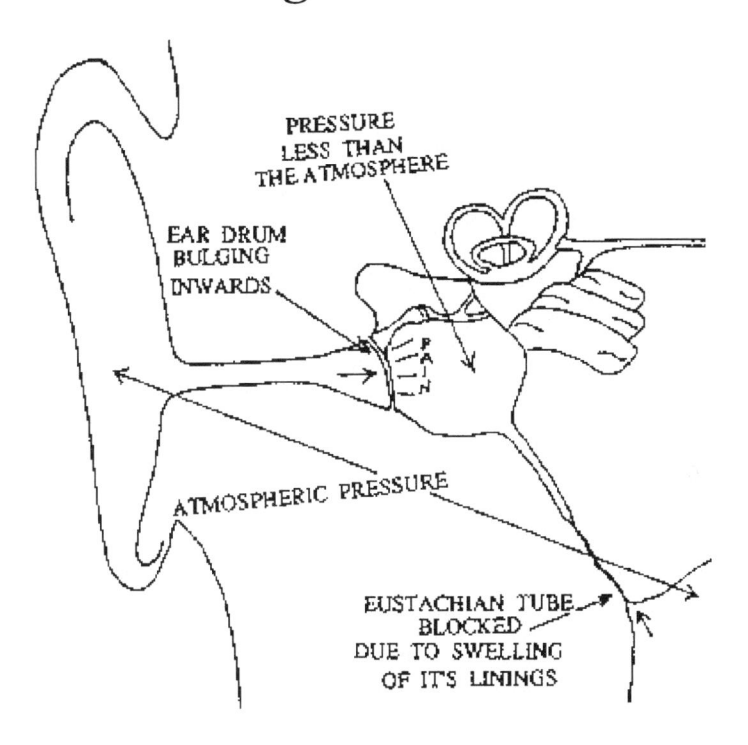

Diagram of the ear showing: PRESSURE LESS THAN THE ATMOSPHERE; EAR DRUM BULGING INWARDS; PAIN; ATMOSPHERIC PRESSURE; EUSTACHIAN TUBE BLOCKED DUE TO SWELLING OF ITS LININGS

Our bodies experience pain and that means we should avoid or stop whatever is causing it. **For freedivers, the most common pain is in the ear drums** and if not alleviated through equalization techniques, can lead to ruptured eardrums.

The mechanism of this pain is the stretching of the eardrum due to the different amount of pressure on the inside and outside. Nerves within the eardrum inform us we have reached 'failure depth' – the depth at which our ears 'fail' to handle the pressure.

Equalization techniques work down to depths of roughly 30 meters but beyond that, the force of compression has reduced the volume of air in our lungs to the point of not having any left for equalization. Advanced divers develop techniques for trapping air in the mouth so that it can be used to offset the pressure in the ears and they can dive deeper.

The lungs, on the other hand, **suffer from the same effects of pressure** but have no nerves to inform the body they are in distress. And also unlike the ears, the lungs are not single membranes but a collection of tiny blood vessels that can rupture in what is called a '*lung squeeze*'. Allowing this to occur over time causes serious injury to the lungs. The only way to reduce this risk is to develop an extremely flexible diaphragm and soft tissues so that they can press harder against the lungs to push back against external pressures.

CHAPTER 9 – FREEDIVING EQUIPMENT

This could be an extremely short chapter since there is technically no need for any equipment to enjoy the sport of freediving. That being said, though, there are a number of items that do make freediving easier and safer. Unlike scuba gear, freediving equipment is rather simple and does not have to cost much money. Most reputable sporting goods shops carry a variety of *masks*, *fins*, *snorkels* and *wet suits* that are suitable for virtually all freediving adventures.

You can, of course, get involved with extra items such as dive computers and watches or high quality under water cameras but they don't really add to the performance of freediving.

Masks

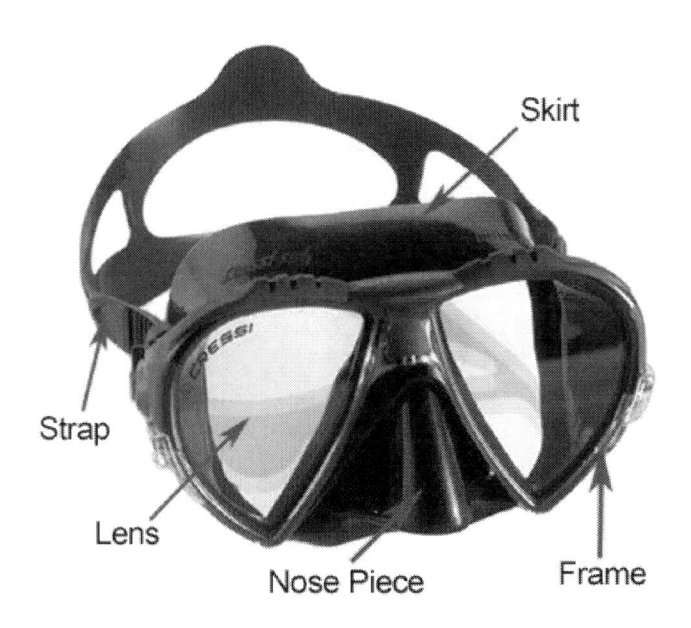

For most freedivers, **a low volume mask** is the most important piece of equipment. The smaller volume of this type of mask makes it easier to equalize in that it does not require as much air to even out the pressure. **Silicone** is the **material** that holds up best to the conditions of salt water and sun and is flexible enough for comfort.

When deciding on a mask, **it is important that the fit is perfect** – no air can escape! One solution to that possible problem is goggles where only the eyes are covered. New technology has led to the creation of fluid goggles that don't have to be equalized. They are filled with saline or liquid silicone and contain several lenses but are still rather expensive.

Facial shape is the key for selecting a diving mask. You should 'try on' a number of different styles, holding the mask gently up to your face with both hands using your thumbs to hold back the skirt slightly. With the mask gently against your face, release your thumbs. Hold the mask in place without applying any extra pressure and check around the edges to see that there is no sign of light showing between your face and the skirt.

Next, inhale gently and see if the mask stays in place against your face without a big breath or using your hands. For men, being clean-shaven is important so there is silicone to skin contact.

The final test is to press the entire frame of the mask firmly against your face using both hands. If there are any spots on the frame or lenses that hit your lips, nose, eyebrows or cheekbones in the store, chances are pretty high that you will feel the same pressure points under water.

Snorkels

Compared to the variety of masks and fins that are available, snorkels are easy to find and can be quite basic. You are simply looking for comfort since you don't want hard plastic pressing into your tongue or gums that could lead to blisters or bleeding. Caps, purge valves and anti-splash components are not necessary and can actually create unneeded drag.

Fins

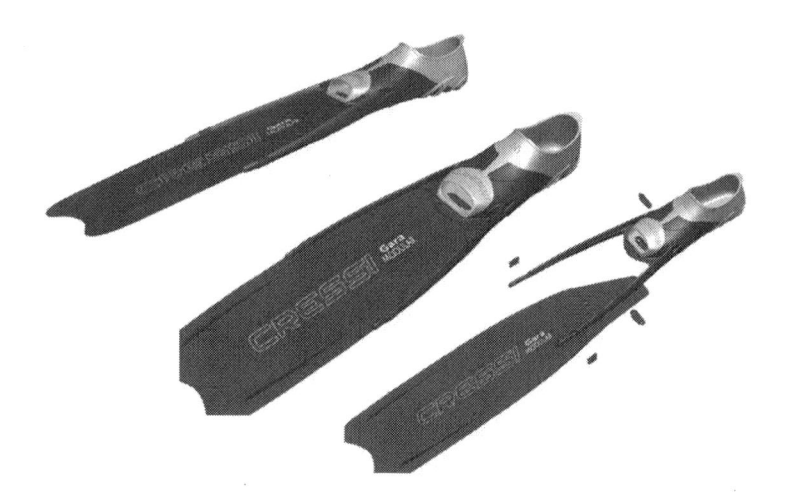

Freediving fins are completely unlike fins used for scuba diving. They are much longer (up to 90 – 100 cm or at least 39 inches) and narrower. Since the propulsion power of the fin is determined by the wave of water that is deflected straight back, manufacturers have created fins with ribs and grooves to deflect the water for maximum efficiency.

The stiffness of the blades is also a matter of choice and depends on the purpose of the fins. For general freediving, soft, flexible fins that have a gentle recoil are the most effective and less fatiguing than stiffer blades. Stiff blades are a better choice for fins for deep diving because they provide more power. They sap energy more quickly and if used for general swimming can cause cramps in the calves and feet. The strength needed to use stiff bladed fins demands a lot from the diver's lower back and can also cause muscle strain.

Fins must fit snugly since they are an extension of the leg and foot of the diver. This provides the greatest thrust without losing power.

Instead of bi-fins, many freedivers have chosen to use a **monofin** due to the greater surface area for more power and lack of drag that occurs between kicks (inter-blade turbulence) with standard fins. A well-coordinated dolphin kick is the main requirement for using a monofin but the results are well worth it, especially since it is thought that this style of finning consumes less oxygen.

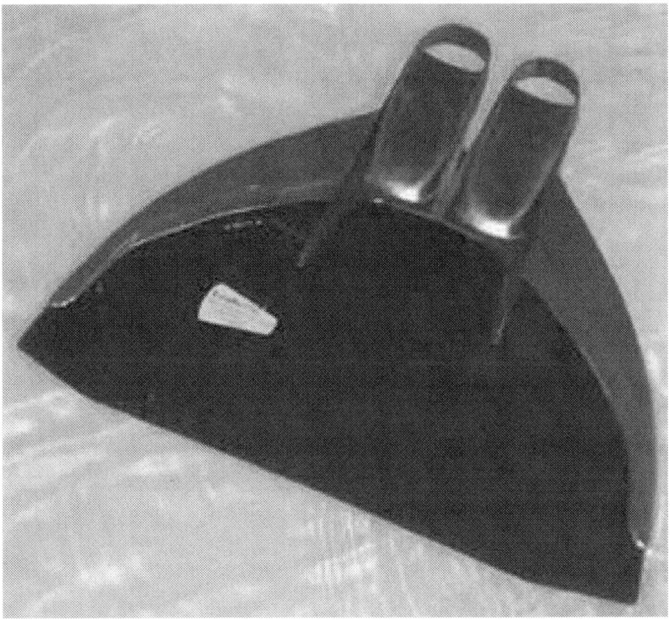

Wetsuits

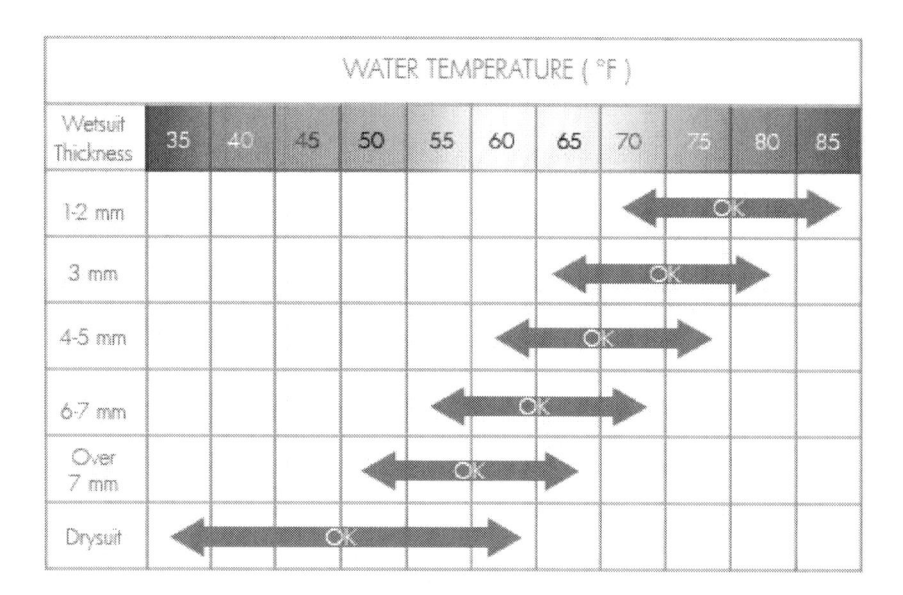

Wetsuit Thickness	35	40	45	50	55	60	65	70	75	80	85
1-2 mm									OK		
3 mm							OK				
4-5 mm						OK					
6-7 mm					OK						
Over 7 mm				OK							
Drysuit	OK										

Water Temperature (°F)

For safety and increased diving performance, it is worth the money to invest in a well-fitted **open cell wetsuit**. This type of suit gently hugs your body like a second skin and provides increased flexibility for proper body positioning and breathing. Another benefit of open cell freedive wetsuits is that they are warmer than standard scuba and surfing wetsuits. Open cell freediving wetsuits provide some buoyancy so you need to properly weight yourself so you can accurately target your neutral buoyancy depth. Personal comfort levels are all different and depend on the environment where you will be diving. In some cases, the only real purpose of the wet suit is to act like a rash guard but in the event of cold water diving, you need to consider a wet suit that is more than 5 mil thick. In general, it's thickness will depend on the temperature of the water you will be diving in.

For the easiest glide through the water, a smooth **neoprene surface** is the best choice. It is also wise to find a suit that is flexible and has a small degree of compression at depth. Really serious freedivers often choose to have a wetsuit custom made to fit perfectly and such suits even come with the arms already in a forward-stretching position.

Boots and Gloves

Neoprene socks and gloves can provide warmth but are also used to protect the hands from coming in contact with something sharp or poisonous. They offer protection from the guide line or other ropes as well. The socks aid in the snug fitting of fins for better control.

Weights

Weights for freediving are, by necessity, as simple as possible. For depth diving the, freediver needs positive buoyancy to make a rapid ascent so weights are not usually needed. In choosing a wetsuit, the freediver uses the least buoyant type available so he does not have to worry about changing pressures and their varying effects on the suit and his buoyancy.

Quick release weight belts may be used so that they can easily be dropped if the diver needs to quickly return to the surface. This is especially important in the event of shallow water blackout – natural buoyancy will continue to bring the compromised diver to the surface where a buddy or spotter can recognize that there is a problem and provide emergency assistance.

Freedivers interested in swimming at a relatively shallow depth to enjoy the environment or take pictures can weight themselves for that specific depth by following these instructions:

- Account for body fat, lung capacity, clothing and equipment and type of water (salt or fresh) and calculate the weight needed for neutral buoyancy at 15 feet. For most people, this will be somewhere between 3% and 5% of their body weight.

- Using small increments of weight, add weight until you reach neutral buoyancy at your desired depth.

As a very general rule of thumb, 1.3 kg (3 pounds) may be enough for a trained freediver without a wetsuit but if wearing a full wetsuit intended for cold water, the same person may need over 10kg (25 pounds).

One major consideration is the material the weight belt is made of. Since compression affects your body and wetsuit, a **rubber belt** is the best choice because it will stay in place and not slide down over your chest and shoulders like a mesh belt can.

Additional Equipment

If you are not involved with a club or a package diving excursion, you should also consider a few different pieces of equipment for safety.

- Just like scuba divers and spear fishermen, carrying a **small knife** that straps to your arm or leg can get you out of some type of entrapment.

- It is also important to mark your diving site with a **flag** if you go out on a kayak or other small float.

- A **lanyard** is important, especially in murky water, to keep you in touch with the line.

Well-Known Brands

Cressi, Esclapez, Mares, Omer, Picasso, and *Sporasub* are among the leaders in providing the best equipment for freediving and can be found at sporting goods shops, dive shops and marinas and online. *Deep Apnea* and *Spierre* are also names for excellent fins.

CHAPTER 10 – SAFETY

It cannot be stated emphatically enough – freediving can be an extremely dangerous activity. Accepting that, there are a number of precautions and guidelines to follow that can minimize the chance of serious problems.

Professional training or instruction is one of the first things that should be considered since learning from someone else's experience can save you some hard lessons. There are numerous clubs that sponsor classes for basic training as well as advanced certification so it is well worth looking into.

Preparation

Safe freediving begins with preparation – physical, mental and organizational. So far, this book has covered the first two components of preparation and now it is time to address the third.

1. **Freediving should never be attempted alone.**

    The danger of drowning is simply too great! The first item to check off, then, is having a buddy if not a group of divers. Each person involved in the dive should be able to handle basic rescue skills and know how to get help for more serious situations.

    - At least one member of the team proficient with CPR and assisted breathing techniques

    - A fully charged cell phone with a signal

    - A dive site that is in close proximity to surface support for emergency rescues

    - Easy access to water, a whistle, a mirror and extra floatation at the dive buoy

2. **Freedivers must be aware of the weather and dive conditions.**

    Rough conditions and bad weather can prove to be quite dangerous for freedivers. The best sites should offer some type of protection from wind or unfavorable surface conditions.

    - Visibility should be adequate so the diving buddy can see the diver. If there is any question, the diver should be attached to the guide line with a lanyard so there is no chance of disorientation causing him to swim away from the line.

    - Time of day is important for two reasons – sharks and other predators feed around dawn and lighting conditions can deteriorate rapidly towards dusk.

    - Know the schedule of the tide and aim for diving between tides. Tides and tide reversals can create strong pull that carry divers away from the shore or boat.

- Avoid strong currents since it makes swimming more difficult and forces the diver to compensate to stay on target.

3. **Stay alert to the surroundings.**

   Boats or other divers can interfere with a dive site and create problems.

   - Always use a buoy and dive flag to alert others to the presence of divers in the water and pay close attention since not all water sport enthusiasts know the meaning of the flag.

   - Don't set buoys too close together (at least 5 m – 15 feet apart) and don't crowd each buoy with more than 3 divers.

   - Watch for bubbles from scuba gear when the site is being shared to avoid collisions.

4. **Double-check all equipment.**

   Improperly-fitting equipment or pieces that have been damaged can create significant problems for freedivers.

Personal Awareness

Just as there is a preparation checklist, there is also a **personal awareness checklist** each diver should internalize for their own safety and well-being.

1. Prepare a dive plan and discuss it with a designated diving buddy

2. Know and accept your limits and never dive after feeling light headed or experiencing LMC

3. **Do not** hyperventilate prior to diving

4. **Never** use air from a scuba tank while diving

5. Remember to **equalize frequently** and don't descend further if you feel pain from pressure

6. Never exhale on the ascent (professionals may release some air right before breaking the surface to facilitate inhaling as soon as they are out of the water

7. Don't stop in the process of ascending and don't try to swim faster

8. Allow yourself adequate rest between dives – it takes a few minutes for oxygenated blood to circulate to all the muscles (rest twice as long as the total time of the previous dive)

9. Maintain hydration prior to and on dive day – keep bottled water at the dive buoy

10. Don't eat too much before a dive but don't dive on an empty stomach

11. **Never** dive if you feel cold, have a fever or infection, if you are tired or depressed, or if you have drugs or alcohol in your system

12. Don't swim past the bottom of a guide line

13. Be prepared to drop your weights if there is a problem and practice releasing the belt and holding it in your hand for the ascent – it will drop if you lose consciousness

14. **Listen to your body** – just because you have reached a certain

depth or time in the past does not mean you will be able to on every dive

15. Know self-rescue techniques: open your eyes, relax, focus on the breathing you will do at the surface, pull yourself up the line and hold or release weights.

The Role of the Buddy Diver

It is critical that all divers know how to perform **deep and shallow water rescues** if a partner experiences a problem. This should be practiced and discussed so that everyone in the group is prepared to do the right thing at the right time. Remember to plan ahead for nearby emergency services and have a cell phone or other means of communication handy. No diver should ever attempt to dive deeper than his buddy is able!

During a freediving excursion, buddies must **communicate clearly with one another**. A maximum depth needs to be determined as well as a 'meeting point' for the ascent, usually about 10 meters (30 feet) below the surface since this is where the greatest likelihood of *samba* or *SWB* occurs. Even without a problem, it is reassuring to a diver to have a buddy meet him on the way up because it provides a sense of well-being that gives the diver confidence and removes fears.

The most important responsibility of the buddy diver is to **maintain visual contact** of the diver, particularly during the ascent. Once the diver ascends to the level of the buddy, the buddy should stay within arm's length of the diver and be prepared to initiate rescue procedures.

The buddy needs to look for bubbles or if the diver stops actively swimming. Even if a diver doesn't need to be rescued, continue to observe him for several minutes after surfacing for irregular breathing, glassy eyes or body tremors. In that event, support the head and keep his mouth and nose out of the water. Never trust that an OK signal means the diver is OK – wait until his breathing is 'normal' or he starts talking before you consider the dive completed safely.

In the event of severe *LMC* (loss of motor control) **or a *blackout*,** the buddy or rescue personnel should:

- Get the diver on his back

- Verbally urge the diver to breathe (do not yell or exhibit panic!)

- Gently pat the diver's cheeks

- If breathing has not resumed, remove mask and blow over diver's face

- After no more than 20 to 30 seconds, perform one CPR blow to see if the problem is a cramp in the epiglottis

- If breathing does not resume, drop weights and get the diver to safe ground and perform CPR

Note: part of training for freedivers should be a basic first aid course that includes instruction in CPR.

If there is any possibility that the diver has aspirated water, take him to a hospital to be checked out and monitored. Secondary drowning and death can occur even as long as 24 hours after an incident!

If a diver requires rescue from a greater depth, the buddy diver should close off the diver's airways for ascent. The most effective way to bring a diver to the surface is to drop all weights, support him by holding him under the jaw and at the back of the head to close the mouth as you use strong kicks to ascend. If another buddy is on the surface, let them take over with resuscitation so you can regain your breath.

Additional Physical Effects of Freediving

For freedivers trying to maximize depth diving or who do not take adequate rest breaks between dives, there are additional physical considerations to take into account. Attributed to decompression sickness, symptoms reported by these divers – including native pearl and sponge divers – include hearing loss, vision changes, dizziness and paralysis, headaches, nausea and sometimes even permanent spinal cord and brain injury.

Even divers who don't descend to great depths can experience these symptoms if they perform repeated descents without adequate rest time in between. The total submersion time during which nitrogen builds up in the blood adds up, especially with the typically rapid ascents of freediving, and the cumulative effect can lead to **neurological DCS** (*decompression sickness*).

To avoid this build-up of nitrogen in the blood, it is important for all freedivers to maintain a ratio of 2 to one for rest time compared to submersion time.

CONCLUSION

Freediving is an amazing sport that offers a tremendous range of physical and emotional rewards. From the competitive drive to push harder, longer and deeper for world records to the almost spiritual connection to the peace and beauty of the sea, freediving offers something for everyone.

Freediving has been a mainstay of life for some cultures for millennia as a significant source of food and the means to gather products to build the economy. Today, the sport is growing tremendously in popularity with many organizations, clubs and 'schools' that provide instruction, certification and freediving excursions all around the world. Whether your main interest is in pool or depth freediving for competition or any of the recreational freediving pursuits, it is easy to find a place to engage in this demanding activity.

Fresh water is just as welcoming for freedivers with plenty of springs and lake depths to explore. It is also a sport that attracts participants who want to challenge the elements to the extreme by diving under ice! With the opportunity to practice freediving in almost any location, it has contributed to better performance in a variety of other sports such as scuba diving, surfing, synchronized swimming and underwater hockey.

In addition to the satisfaction freedivers experience through participation in the sport, there is the added benefit of tremendous improvement in physical fitness, general health and mental outlook. With the range of cross training exercises, meditation techniques and yoga or Pilates, and a focus on proper nutrition and a healthy lifestyle, freedivers thrive much more than the brief periods of time they are actually in the water.

Equipment is of little concern for the most part since wetsuits, fins, masks and snorkels are standard gear for other purposes. For that reason, freediving may be considered to be more economical than other sports, unless you choose to travel the world for competitions or the best underwater scenery.

Safety is the most important consideration for freedivers because of the inherent dangers of loss of motor control or shallow water blackout, not to mention ruptured ear drums. To truly enjoy the sport, those who are interested should make sure that they understand the issues that make it potentially dangerous.

There is no time like the present to take the plunge and experience the excitement of freediving. With the suggestions in this book and advice or instruction from certified freedivers, you can quickly and easily accomplish breath holds and freedives that will spark your interest and draw you back for more!

ABOUT THE AUTHOR

Mike McGuire has always loved the ocean. Growing up beside the ocean, he had endless opportunities to scuba and fish, becoming acquainted at an early age with fishing and freediving. He began fishing with his father, at a very young age, enjoying the spray of the water over the side of the boat. Once he was old enough to scuba dive, his father (a scuba instructor) began taking Mike on freediving excursions, and once he was comfortable in the water, they brought along the spearguns. Not only did he enjoy spending time with his father, he genuinely enjoyed swimming in the ocean and the sport of hunting down the perfect fish for dinner.

Ever since he was a boy, Mike has spent the majority of his life in the water, traveling all over the world to fish in the best waters, and talking to other spearfishermen and freedivers about their equipment and technique. As he has accumulated this information, he began testing it out, documenting it, making a note of what was sound advice, and what didn't hold water. Through years of trial and error, he began to uncover the best places to fish, the best depths, and the best freediving and spearfishing equipment, even winning a few competitions along the way.

As he spoke with those experienced in this activity, he saw a need for a book that could not only quickly teach men the sport of spearfishing and freediving, but also provide a safety, gear, and technique refresher to those who had been diving and fishing for years.

All of the advice in his book has been thoroughly field tested by Mike McGuire himself. This compilation of knowledge is a result of years of experience and working with other spearfishing and freediving experts. Throughout this process, Mike became especially fascinated with the easiest way to teach others to spearfish. As he talked with people that had never done the sport, he realized that most of them were daunted by the concept, and that it seemed too complicated to learn.

Over the years, however, he had come to understand that spearfishing and freediving were actually easy sports, something that could be easily learned and passed on, if those who wished to learn it were provided with only the best information and advice. His philosophy has always been to keep it simple and to keep it clean. His long process of trial and error has taught Mike that it is alright to fail, as long as you keep trying and don't complicate a simple sport with too much flash and flair.

All of his knowledge, and years of expertise have been brought together in one easy to follow, fun to read book.